Robert Dunlop

Life and Times of a Legend

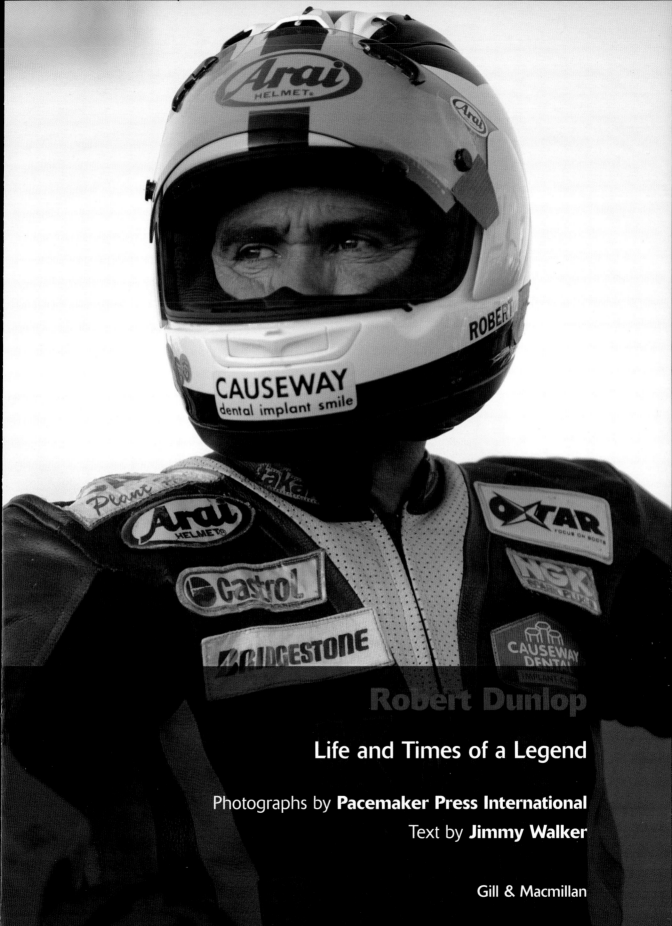

Robert Dunlop

Life and Times of a Legend

Photographs by **Pacemaker Press International**

Text by **Jimmy Walker**

Gill & Macmillan

Gill & Macmillan Ltd

Hume Avenue, Park West, Dublin 12

with associated companies throughout the world

www.gillmacmillan.ie

Text © Jimmy Walker 2008

Photographs and captions © Pacemaker Press International 2008

978 07171 4596 6

Design and print origination by Design Image

Printed and bound in Italy by L.E.G.O. SpA

This book is typeset in Delta Jaeger 9 on 15.

The paper used in this book comes from the wood pulp of managed forests. For every tree felled, at
least one tree is planted, thereby renewing natural resources.

A CIP catalogue record for this book is available from the British Library.

1 3 5 4 2

>> Robert Dunlop salutes the crowd as he sets out on a parade lap on the John Player Special Rotary Norton at the Ulster Grand Prix at Dundrod in 2003.

>> Robert Dunlop in action at the Dundrod 150 in 2002.

Contents >>

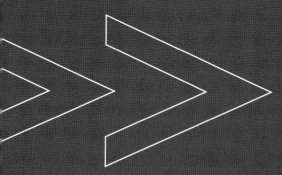

Acknowledgments >>

Photographs © Pacemaker Press International by Stephen Davison, Maurice Montgomery, Clifford McClean, Trevor Armstrong, Charles McQuillan and David Collister.

Acknowledgments from Jimmy Walker

I would like to thank my wife, Iris, for her unstinting support during the writing of this book.

My daughter, Shelly, for producing the manuscript in such a short time.

Louise Dunlop, widow of Robert Dunlop, for being abundantly helpful, especially in the immediate period after Robert's accident, when no question bothered her.

Liam Beckett for his fund of background stories to Robert's career.

Willis Marshall for supplying background material to Robert's career during his time as manager.

Barry Symmons who provided material on Robert's time at Norton when Barry was manager of the team.

>> Robert Dunlop at the
Temple 100 in 1998.

Chapter 1

Robert Dunlop pulls into the pits on the Hanna
250cc Honda during the first North West 200
practice session on the opening night of practice
for the 2008 race. This was the only lap Robert
completed on the bike at the event, as he was
killed at Mather's Cross on the first lap
of the second practice session on
Thursday evening.

The sound
of silence

It was the day the music died, and all that was left was the sound of silence.

Shortly after 10 p.m. on 15 May 2008, Robert Dunlop—who, despite his small stature, had always stood 10 feet tall in the eyes of the motorcycling faithful—gulped his last breath and died as the result of a practice smash at his beloved North West 200.

In many ways it was an ironic, even poignant, death for Dunlop, who was riding over the seaside course where he had set up the record of sixteen wins and where he had no equals. In addition, he was riding in the 250cc class for the first time since his horrific crash in the Isle of Man in 1994, from which he made the most miraculous recovery in the history of road racing.

To add another twist to the story, Robert crashed in front of his son William, who was practising at the same time. It was a shattering and unlikely end to a great career, which a few days earlier had seemed vibrant. Dunlop was looking forward to pouring out his thoughts and achievements over the years in a book. Sadly, after the tragedy of 15 May, while his story can still be told the great man is no longer here to read it. Nor will he be able to hear the tunes of glory that greeted his son Michael two days later in the same North West 200 class, which incredibly saw a result that no scriptwriter could have envisaged.

In fact his two sons, Michael and William, turned up unexpectedly to race on the Saturday, and most of the huge crowd of 100,000 were put into a state of amazement and disbelief as they saw the two young Dunlops on the starting line.

>> Michael Dunlop chats to his father, Robert, on the grid moments before the start of the North West 200 practice session in which Robert lost his life.

>> Michael Dunlop leads John McGuinness at York hairpin during the 250cc race at the 2008 North West 200. Michael won the race just two days after his father, Robert, was killed during practice for the same race.

>> Robert Dunlop with his three sons, Daniel, Michael and William.

But to win the race, as Michael did, was something else. Though many officials had tried to dissuade him from racing so soon after his father's death, Michael would have none of it. William was spared racing when his bike seized shortly after the start, but Michael went on to a glory that took the motorcycling world by storm.

The Dunlops, of course, were born for success in the fast lane and for showing that intense, frightening attention to detail that put them above all others.

>> Robert Dunlop carries his brother Joey's coffin at his funeral in 2000.

Joey Dunlop—the biggest name in motorcycling—was a hero whose death in a crash in Estonia in 2000 shocked the sporting world and brought motorcycling in Ireland shuddering to a halt. More than five thousand people were at Joey's funeral in July 2000, and everyone secretly hoped we would never see its like again. But, tragically, Robert's funeral followed eight years later, and again the fans turned out to pay their respects.

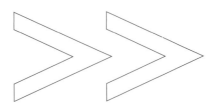

>> Joey and Robert Dunlop sit side by side on the 125cc grid at the 1990 Cookstown 100.

Robert and Joey Dunlop in the Isle of Man TT winners' enclosure in 2000 after Joey won the Ultra-Lightweight TT and Robert was third. It was Joey's last TT win and the last time the brothers raced against each other.

Robert and Joey Dunlop were two brothers who were set apart not just from the rest of the motorcycle travelling circus but from each other. That's what made them great. Joey was always glued to the bike and had little time for small talk, while at the other end of the spectrum Robert couldn't talk enough. He was an interviewer's dream; but there were more than quips in Robert's battery of one-liners. He had deep feelings, which he showed with this tribute to Joey he wrote in 2001 after a trip to a remote place in the Republic where he took time to sort things out in his head and think about what his gifted brother had meant to him. Entitled "The Joey I Knew," Robert's message to fans, written as a foreword to Joey's biography, said:

"Most people saw Joey for his brilliance on a motorcycle but to me he was just a brother, no different from my brother Jim but with a different personality and after all that's what makes us what we are. Joey and I shared the same blood group but we always shared a similar passion for racing and this was what drove Joey on. I am grateful that he had this special passion and that is why he would never have stopped racing; it's also the reason I can't either. I am glad my father understands and recognises this, for it's this passion that makes a man great.

>> Robert Dunlop (Norton) follows brother Joey (Honda) round Metropole in the Superbike race at the North West 200 in 1991.

"On that devastating day, Sunday 2 July when Joey was killed, Jim and I arrived at a small house in Union Street which we called home in the town of Ballymoney along with my four sisters to break the news about Joey.

"Mum was just coming home with her little dog after a walk when I met her just outside the front door. I couldn't tell Mum—how could I? I just said, 'I've a bit of bad news,' and Mum replied heartily, 'What's wrong with you now?' But it became devastatingly clear what was up as we entered the living room and she saw the looks on the faces of her family. I will never forget my mother's weeping at the loss of her son. I wept for my mother that day for I was chilled to the bone. Joey was a very deep person at times but also a happy-go-lucky old-fashioned type who loved to laugh and fool with people. When I was a teenager I looked up to him as my big brother and I suppose I tried hard to impress him. Joey knew this so he would dare me to do anything and talk me into going first. Then he would have a good laugh when I would fall on my face.

>> Robert Dunlop (4, Norton) and his brother Joey (3, Honda) ride side by side around the Roundabout at the North West 200 in 1991.

"I miss the fun and the craic. I miss his stories of his adventures all over the world. I miss the great battles we had on the track but I do have my memories and they will go on forever.

"I can no longer look beside me in a race and see Joey's helmet and his piercing eyes inside. I just talk to him now and I am sure he can still hear me."

Louise Dunlop, Robert's widow, was highly impressed by this piece of writing. She pointed out that Robert went into a monastic mood of silence for the next three weeks. "He didn't want to go anywhere or do anything," she said. "He was just wrapped up in himself and thoughts of Joey. When I think back to those days and the way Robert handled Joey's death I must say that he couldn't have gone out and raced two days afterwards, as the case with his two sons following Robert's death. But then everyone is made differently, and Robert especially would lose himself in deep thoughts.

Robert Dunlop and his twin sister, Margaret, as children.

A very early racing paddock shot of Robert Dunlop. He is wearing his brother Joey's leathers.

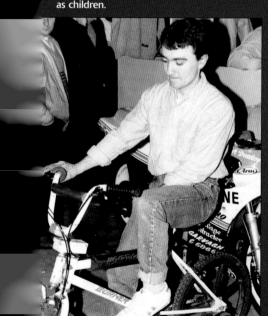

A young Robert Dunlop at a motorcycle show in the 1980s.

Robert Dunlop.

"I knew he would never retire. He often told me this, and many times he mentioned that he would go on racing until the end came. I leave the meaning of that up to interpretation. But take it from me, Robert Dunlop had no wish to sit on the sidelines and watch racing, even with his sons taking part. It was just the way he was made. As he told me often enough, 'I do what I do.'"

>> Robert Dunlop kisses his wife, Louise.

Louise Dunlop first met Robert when she was enjoying a working holiday from her home in Norfolk. A woman who knew all about working with horses, she decided to take a six-month break and work for Templepatrick Auctions in Co. Antrim. She worked in the yard and in the auction and met Ken Dundee, a local car salesman, and Barbara Blair, a woman in the same trade. She shared a flat with Barbara, and Dundee was later to become a sponsor of Robert Dunlop.

However, Louise did not know in those days that her first encounter with the "Mighty Atom" was when Ken Dundee gave her tickets for the Mid-Antrim Club prizegiving at the Country House Hotel, Doagh, in the 1980s. Among those at one table was an impish Robert Dunlop, and Louise told me: "He wasn't very impressive. And he was also

>> An early racing shot of Robert Dunlop in action at Aghadowey circuit, Co. Londonderry in the early 80s. Note the Joey Dunlop replica helmet he is wearing.

very small, so much so I had to kick off my high-heel shoes to dance with him. But I liked him, and the affection grew as time went on. We had a great circle of friends. We would party, race and come home. We were constantly together, and Robert and I were eventually married.

"I had grown up with horses and had never been involved with motorbikes. My mother and my grandfather dealt in horses at Swaffham, and the Dunlop set—or rather the Ulster motorcycle set—were all new as far as I was concerned.

>> Robert Dunlop with his wife, Louise, and one of her horses at their Ballymoney, Co. Antrim, home in 2001.

"The first time I saw Robert race was at Carrowdore in Co. Down, and eventually Robert and I were inseparable when it came to the paddock clan, who followed all the boys on bikes.

"Robert's life changed when our first son, William, was born. He had to be more serious about getting a career. While everyone enjoyed road racing, Robert had to earn some real money, and this he did through steel erecting. He worked for many years at this business, even in the days when he became a top road racer. He and Joey would go down to a building site and do a job at which they were highly skilled."

Robert Dunlop and his son William in the Tandragee 100 paddock in 1987.

Louise's first home with Robert was a little cottage on the outskirts of Ballymoney, and this place is still there. At least the garage is, for Robert built this adjunct to the house and it is still standing as something of a memorial to the talents of Robert, not only as a motorcyclist but as a builder. "As I remember it, he knocked the building up in record time; but then life was tough in those days. It was a lot different from what it is now. Everyone had to do their bit and you didn't get ahead without hard work. That was why Robert continued to concentrate on improving the excellence of anything he did. He was a brilliant mechanic, as everybody who knew him would agree, but he didn't get on 100 per cent with all the motorcycling community. It has been well documented that the top-class road racer Phillip McCallen, who came on the scene in the 125cc class in the 1980s, was a rider whom Robert was wary of. Robert kept himself to himself, and so did Phillip. On the roads they had a highly focused confrontation from race to race, but such was their personality that they never palled up, as the rest of us did."

>> Robert Dunlop (Ducati) leads Phillip McCallen (Honda) in the Superbike race at the Ulster Grand Prix in 1993.

<< Robert Dunlop with his wife, Louise, and one of his TT trophies.

Phillip always looked as though he was riding within an inch of disaster and was very much up for success. Robert knew this and was well aware that Phillip would give him no chance of success if he could get away with it. Each rubbed the other up the wrong way; but that's the way it goes.

>> Robert Dunlop on the podium after winning the Superbike race at the 1990 North West 200, flanked by Phillip McCallen and Eddie Laycock. Also included are Miss North West 200 and the Hutchinson brothers, race sponsors.

I remember one day Phillip trying to pass and going on the outside, spraying up loose stones as Robert was alongside. This urgency to win was typical of McCallen in those days—but let's face it: Robert was just as keen to succeed as Phillip was.

Perhaps the nadir of their disagreement came in 1992 after a well-documented incident at the Ulster Grand Prix. The introduction of a new chicane at the start and finish area marked the first major change to the circuit since Leathemstown Bridge was dropped from the layout in 1966. The chicane was not popular with fans and competitors and lowered lap times by about six seconds.

23

The meeting got off to the worst possible start when the opening 250cc class was stopped on the third lap and then abandoned after a serious accident at the tree-lined Ireland's Corner involving McCallen and Steve Johnston. McCallen escaped lightly—nothing worse than a broken shoulder—but 31-year-old Johnston from Whitley Bay was killed instantly.

The problem as I saw it in the aftermath of the accident was that Robert Dunlop held an impromptu press conference to tell everyone that in his view McCallen had been at fault. Whether or not Robert should have said such a thing remains to be seen, but he was obviously buzzed up following the incident, and probably had he cooled off he would have operated in a more composed manner.

Robert Dunlop (12, Norton) lines up alongside Johnny Rea (17, Honda), Trevor Nation (5, Norton), Phillip McCallen (Honda), Carl Fogarty (4, Honda) and Joey Dunlop (3, Honda) at the start of the Superbike race at the 1990 North West 200.

Anyway, McCallen wasn't too enamoured at looking as though he might be involved in a blame game. "I had a superb North West 200 and Isle of Man TT that year, and at the Ulster Grand Prix I was in pole position for every race I started. At the time I was beginning to win road races no matter who else was there. I had the machinery and I was determined.

"On a long day like that you have to pace yourself. I learnt that after the North West. There is no point in putting all your energy into the first race when there is plenty more to come.

"Brian Reid was leading and I had moved into second, with Steve Johnston third and Robert Dunlop in fourth or fifth place. We were just getting settled in, and I knew if Brian Reid set the early pace I would stay with him and let him do the work out in front for a lap or two.

"We went into Ireland Corner and I felt a bump or a bang, like something had hit the back of my bike. My bike went sideways right across the road. I remember fighting it the whole way along the top of the bank or hedge, trying to hold on to it. That was it. I was knocked out. I remember nothing until I woke up in hospital.

"I was pretty smashed up. I didn't know anyone else had been involved in the crash until the next day.

"My mother and family were there. They had been with me at the hospital all that night. I knew something was wrong but I didn't know what it was until they told me another rider had been killed, and that I was being blamed.

"That day I was racing number 1 and my bike was green and white. Steve Johnston was riding number 9, my usual number, and his bike was also green and white, so people got mixed up about what they saw and what they thought had happened. At the inquest some people gave evidence that I had caused the accident, and some people said I hadn't. A home video taken at Ireland's Corner didn't show the point of impact but it showed our positions on the road a spilt second before the impact. This showed that I couldn't have taken Steve off. The inquest agreed that it was a racing accident."

The remainder of that meeting was held in sombre circumstances, but Robert Dunlop became the hero of the hour when he had a double and won a victory for Norton, which was the first for the British machine at the Ulster since 1965.

> I was pretty smashed up. I didn't know anyone else had been involved in the crash until the next day.

Norton's first TT success for nineteen years had come with Steve Hislop riding to victory in the Senior and with Robert Dunlop third. Dunlop then rolled back the years with a pair of start-to-finish Superbike wins at the Ulster. With Joey Dunlop a first-lap retirement at the pits after his RC30 developed valve trouble, Robert galloped the Norton into the lead. It took Dunlop three laps to shake the persistent Steve Warn and to ease clear of his challengers. By then Warn had his own problems, in the shape of Ian Duffus, who was mounting a strong challenge on the Kawasaki. Despite riding for most of the distance with a broken steering damper, Duffus almost claimed the runner-up spot. However, it was Dunlop who took the win, with ten seconds to spare.

Dunlop started favourite for the second Superbike race, and it appeared as though he had Nick Jefferies as his main opponent. Dunlop once again struck into the lead at the start. Jefferies broke clear of a closing pack of Robert Holden, Ian Simpson, Ian Duffus and Alan Irwin, who kept the Norton firmly in their sights.

>> Robert Dunlop leads his Norton teammate Trevor Nation around Metropole
during the Superbike race at the 1991 North West 200.

As they began the final lap, Dunlop was only in front by a mere second, but he seemed to have that bit extra in reserve and raised the pace to win by 2.2 seconds. He said afterwards: "At that time Norton were starting to get into financial difficulties. John Kennedy was my personal sponsor and he decided to bring the team over for the North West 200 and the Ulster Grand Prix.

"I had been riding the bike in England on short circuits. There is quite a bit of difference between Dundrod and any other course. Dundrod is a very smooth circuit: a lot of fast corners, 'knee on the road' type of stuff. At that stage I was used to scratching and it suited me.

"I controlled both races at the Ulster, went a bit faster when I had to and didn't have any trouble in either of them."

In the mid-1990s Joey Dunlop was the king, but he was injured one year, which meant he had to miss the TT, and Robert was looking for a Honda to race. He asked Louise to speak to Bob McMillan, the Honda boss, to see what she could do. Louse said: "I said to McMillan that Robert will win the race for him. This was the 125cc, where Robert was particularly successful. Bob said, 'Never mind, Louise, we'll win it anyway.' As it turned out, McCallen got the bike but Andy McManamy from Cookstown stepped forward and gave Robert a new Honda. Believe it or not, Robert not only smashed the lap record but won the race. What a day!"

Robert was enjoying his success in the Isle of Man, a place where he had suffered a lot of injury. Probably his first encounter and near miss was in 1985 when he crashed at the eleventh milestone and suffered internal injuries and broken ribs and ended up in intensive care. Louise said: "Robert drifted in and out of consciousness, and we thought we lost him. All the family were there, hoping against hope that he would pull through. How often had we been in that position, with Robert hovering on the brink of eternity."

His uncle Dick Barclay decided to ring a faith healer, Matt Gibson, who had so often helped Joey. Well, Matt came to the Isle of Man, and all was well. Robert pulled through, and it was on to the next hazard in a hectic racing life.

Louise added that Robert's history of accidents had begun long before his road-racing career. "Not many know this, but when he was only seventeen he was driving home late at night along Frosses Road, which leads eventually to Ballymoney and Coleraine, at the famous bit where the trees cross the road and make an archway. Robert crashed into one of these otherwise picturesque pieces of nature and broke his neck. He was in traction in the Royal Victoria Hospital in Belfast. He carried the scar for the rest of his life. He was in a van when it came off the road and hit that tree, but the accident left him with a weak neck for the rest of his life."

Robert Dunlop in the Medd Honda leathers at the 1994 North West 200.

>> Robert Dunlop in action in the Lightweight TT at Rhencullen in 1991 in the Isle of Man.
Photograph by David Collister.

>> Robert Dunlop in action at the Isle of Man TT in 1994 on the Medd Honda RC45 before his accident at Ballaugh. Photograph by David Collister.

Such was the amount of injury that dogged Dunlop through his career. Davy Wood, one of his pals and mentors, believed that Robert should give up racing and concentrate on the Grand Prix sport, but this never really took off. Robert was in love with racing between the hedges and trees; he would never agree that he would win a world title on the track.

He had a friend called Carl Fogarty who was set to go on to greater things and become World Superbike Champion. I always thought that Fogarty was an arrogant type, but Robert admired him, even though they came from opposite sides of the tracks. Carl came from a wealthy family, while Robert had more humble beginnings.

Still, in 1991 Robert produced the goods on the track when he won the British Championship. I'll never forget his win in the Austrian GP, when he was disqualified some hours later because he hadn't carried a weight on the bike that he should have. However, he was awarded the prize money, so that was some consolation.

In a previous round at Mondello, near Dublin, he ended up barred from the race because he parted company with the track during practice and failed to avoid some bollards. There was nothing straightforward with Robert, and he was sent home in high dudgeon.

"Arguably the biggest crash and the one that was life-threatening to a great extent happened in 1994. This is the incident that changed his life and his style of racing. It also ended in a law suit, and fortunately we were successful."

>> Robert Dunlop in action at the Metropole on the Medd RC45 Honda in the 1994 North West 200.

In the Formula 1 TT Robert was riding the Medd Honda on which he had scored a double at the North West 200. Then, while well placed in the TT, Robert's Honda ran into trouble in Ballagh Bridge and the back wheel disintegrated. Robert hit a wall and injured his arm and leg so much that surgeons said afterwards that the limbs would be useless. In fact it was reckoned that if Robert had been a younger man the limbs would have been amputated.

>> The Medd Honda photographed after the crash at Ballaugh in 1994 during the Senior TT. The rear wheel, which had collapsed, causing the accident, can be clearly seen.

Robert Dunlop arrived home in Belfast later that summer, and his recovery continued in Dundonald Hospital, where I used to visit him daily.

I often asked him at that time if he was going to continue with road racing, but it seemed that the answer would be obvious. No-one could have experienced the outcome of a horrific crash and still want to go on. We used to talk about the future, and I remember him lying on the bed like a broken rag doll. At the same time he was a great one for a chat and from time to time he would join me in a cigarette—smoking wasn't frowned on in those days—and we discussed what his future would be. At that time he had no idea of the barriers that would lie ahead when looking for some assistance and understanding of his position.

>> Robert Dunlop recovers in hospital after his crash at the
1994 Isle of Man TT.

➤ Robert Dunlop recovers from his Isle of Man TT crash injuries in 1994 at his Ballymoney home with one of his Great Danes.

For Robert Dunlop was one rider who had to race in order to live. It was his life; and even the thought that he was hopefully going to make some money in an impending court case made no difference.

Regarding the court case, Robert was eventually encouraged to go ahead and sue Stewart Medd of the Medd Honda company, which in turn sued Medd. That's the way it was, and Dunlop had to settle for the fact that he would be suing Stewart. As the case went on, lots of unpleasant facts emerged, one of which was when his fellow-riders Steve Parrish and Roger Burnett took the stand for the insurance company and against Robert.

Louise said: "We were astounded when Parrish said that Robert would not have been a good enough rider to have competed in a World Superbike Championship. Robert's point was that the crash had ruined his career, but Parrish gave the impression that there was no career to ruin.

"We had sold our house at Ballynacree. This had happened under my direction while Robert was on the operating table. The house was sold to a man from Donegal, and when he realised it Robert was furious. But we just had no money and we needed every penny we could get.

37

"Eventually Robert decided to settle out of court, and he received £750,000, but we owed furious amounts of money and we had very little left to take home."

Robert Dunlop always had great faith in Dundonald Hospital, near Belfast. In 1991 he rode in the Isle of Man TT after yet another crash and breaking his collarbone at a British Champion meeting at Donington Park. Louise said: "He was engaged in a battle with Rob Orne when he fell off and was taken to hospital. He phoned me and told me he wanted the Ulster Hospital to see him. Mr McAfee, the surgeon, who knew him well and who later helped in 1994, operated on the collarbone to get him back in business, and believe it or not he appeared at the TT a couple of days later to try and pass a medical. He never let on that he was in pain following his crash, and when it came to doing press-ups for the doctors to prove his fitness he was still able to do so, despite the sweat running down his brow. I will never forget how he got through that medical. It was sheer determination, and he went on to win two TTs in the only time of his career. That's guts for you.

> Robert loved to race and he felt that even on television and having his face beamed into every household he would still miss the buzz of the race.

"Robert was a shining example to other sportsmen, and I remember the jockey Jim Lambe having broken his neck at a point-to-point in Co. Down. Lambe was brought to our house by a good friend, Marshall Fleming, who was a big man in the point-to-point world, and he brought Lambe to see Robert and show what could be done with will power. Lambe looked undecided as to what should happen, and I pointed out to Robert that it wasn't just a question of going back to racing: Lambe had to pass a doctor and receive a licence to ride, and this was not likely.

"It turned out that Lambe didn't go back to race riding but turned to training and has since had a very successful career.

"Robert often asked me what he should do if he gave up riding and I said, 'Why aren't you involved with media—you are good at being a pundit and a bit like John McEnroe. Like McEnroe, you wouldn't let people sit back and do nothing. You would be direct and to the point until you received a proper answer.' Robert thought about this for long enough and on some occasions would come to me and ask if it would work if he joined commentators on television and radio. But the bottom line was that Robert loved to race and he felt that even on television and having his face beamed into every household he would still miss the buzz of the race.

"That's probably why he went on so long, but we will never know what he was feeling on the night of the 15th of May 2008."

>> Robert Dunlop on the Loctite Yamaha at the Sunflower trophy meeting at Kirkistown, Co. Down, in 1991.

Chapter 2 >>>

Pull up your socks!

>> Robert Dunlop in action at the Roundabout on the O'Kane RC30 Honda in the 1989 North West 200.

Pull up your socks! is an exhortation usually given to those athletes who give the impression of not trying too hard. But no-one could say this about Robert Dunlop, who broke every bone in his body in trying to achieve worldwide fame and give the best of this ability to his fans—that is, until 1989, when he had no socks to pull up at all.

Liam Beckett, former Ballymoney soccer star and later coach, tells some wonderful stories about Dunlop during the twenty years when Dunlop and Beckett were high rollers on the road-racing and short-circuit scene. Beckett joined Dunlop in 1986, as he said, mainly because Robert was a fellow Ballymoney man but also because motorcycling was to him as big a challenge as football.

Eventually, in 1989 the pair hit the jackpot when Dunlop won the Macau Grand Prix and finished ahead of his arch-rival Phillip McCallen, who was second. Beckett still recalls those days, but his main memory is of the after-race presentation, when Dunlop ended up with no socks on his feet, all because of lack of thought beforehand. "None of us had the slightest idea that Robert would win at Macau," said Beckett. "As a result, when we were told by Mike Trimby—the organiser of the race and the Englishman who brought a party of riders over every year—that we had to wear an evening suit, we were not pleased, to say the least. Robert couldn't understand it and said, 'Am I going to get a tuxedo for this function at the last minute in Macau? Where do I go to get one?'

"But Robert was never short of ideas and he grabbed a rickshaw driver and got him to take him to the nearest tailor. The driver passed through all red lights on the way, and eventually Robert was measured for his suit. Robert was always a small man, and I used to call him Mr Five Feet Two. That being the case, he was surprised to find that his normal size was a bit small for Macau, and he had to order a medium suit, to which he replied: 'I'm a bigger man than I am at home!'

"So Robert had to get back for the presentation and now had his suit. However, there were more complications, for he had no clean socks and had no time to get some. It was all a bit of a mix-up and a rush, but at the end of the day I told Robert that he couldn't have my socks, for I needed them for the function, so Robert said, 'I've got an idea. I'll not wear any socks at all, and the bottoms of the trousers will hide my ankles, while the top of the shoes will hide the rest of my feet.' Brilliant.

"So off we went to the winners' prize distribution, and we were mixing with the likes of Eddie Irvine and Martin Donnelly, who had been taking part in the car race for F3, which was at the same meeting as the motorbike event. This was the first time I had met Irvine. I must say I found him very likeable, but of course Irvine was far removed from the big time in those days and probably later he might not have taken Robert and myself under his notice. That's just a thought anyway.

>> Robert Dunlop celebrates after winning the 125cc European championship race at Kirkistown in 1993.

43

>> John McGuinness and Robert Dunlop have some fun at the
Centenary TT Champions Gala Dinner in the Isle of Man in 2007.

"But we're back to Robert's problems with his socks and hoped that no-one would notice that he wasn't wearing any. Then the inevitable happened and what we had feared. Mike Trimby and his men suggested that Robert, Irvine and the rest should sit down and be photographed by the press. I was sitting beside Mike Trimby's wife, and she looked towards me and said in hushed tones, 'Does Robert have no socks?' I pretended I didn't know what she meant, but it was quite clear that Robert's ankles were showing and that he had no socks in his attire. Mrs Trimby added, 'I never saw anything like this before.' I agreed and tried to calm her down by reassuring her that something might have gone wrong. Anyway, we got through the evening all right. Robert had won, and he was so delighted he showed the trophy to everyone and said, 'This is the one race which Joey has never won. I'm one up on him now. Have a look at the list of winners: it's tremendous to figure among them.'

>> Joey and Robert Dunlop on the podium in the Isle of Man in 2000 after Joey won the Ultra-Lightweight TT and Robert was third. It was Joey's last TT win and the last time the brothers raced against each other.

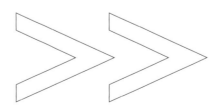

47

Robert Dunlop competing in the 125cc race at the British Grand Prix, Donington, in 1992.

"Meanwhile we had the problem of the socks, which we had wriggled out of, but everyone remembered what had happened and there is no doubt that Robert and I were both embarrassed. This saga continued the following year, in 1990, when at the breakfast launch of the Macau race Trimby produced a packet of socks for each of us and said not to lose them!

"Robert was very popular in Macau. He had a way with him, and he got on the right side of a Japanese businessman, who invited us for supper. We went for dinner in his limousine, which took us to his house. The next thing, we were offered a glass each of snake wine. I nearly died, because I could see the snakes inside the jar. Robert said to me not to sip it because it would turn my stomach. The plan was to knock it back with one gulp, which we did and then fell down on the floor.

"The Japanese businessman was impressed that Robert and I had shown such a liking for his wine and offered to give us more, since we weren't drunk, but we decided not to bother and to defer his invitation to further celebration!"

Beckett could go on for hours about himself and Robert in their heyday. He told me that he regarded Robert's best performance as that of 1991, when he won the British 125cc Championship. Dunlop not only had wins all over the place but broke an amazing number of lap records. The centrepiece of that season was of course, as mentioned earlier, when he went on to win the TT despite suffering a broken collarbone two days earlier, but what is not generally known is that Beckett packed nappies around Robert's ribs so as to ease the pain.

>> Robert Dunlop is named Enkalon Irish Motorcyclist of the Year for the second time in 1991.

Another win that Beckett remembers vividly is the 125cc Ulster GP, when Robert just got the better of his brother Joey and Mike Lofthouse, who was sadly killed later in the Isle of Man. Lofthouse won the admiration of Joey, who said at the time that he would turn into a great rider. But that three-way battle in the Ulster GP is something that is still remembered long after those days of the 1990s.

Back to Macau, and Beckett has still plenty to talk about. He recalled to me the famous incident when he and Robert were issued four breakfast coupons instead of two. "I said to Robert, 'What do you think we should do?' Robert told me that as north Antrim men we should grab the tickets and say nothing. The plan was to use the extra tickets for dinner. So we went down to the kitchen for dinner and offered these breakfast tickets, and all hell broke loose. All of a sudden the whole of the kitchen was filled with irate Chinamen who insisted that we had made a mistake. Eventually we had to give up and join the riders' conference given by Trimby in another part of the hotel.

"Needless to say, Trimby pointed out the problem with the breakfast coupons and said it had come to his notice that two members of the party had tried to double up the coupons with dinner and that this was not acceptable. Robert stood up and looked across and said to me, 'I wonder who would do that. What an awful person; I hope he's caught.' To which I replied, 'I agree, Robert. That's the sort of thing that should be stamped out on these trips.' Needless to say, we heard no more about it."

Robert Dunlop leads the 125cc race at the Ulster Grand Prix, Dundrod, in 1993 from Mick Lofthouse and his brother Joey.

Robert Dunlop shakes hands with Grand Prix legend Giacomo Agostini before the start of their parade lap at Portrush during the North West festival in 2001.

Apart from Macau, Dunlop also rode in Europe, and at Monza he crashed in the warm up lap for the 125cc World Championship race. He dislocated his hip, and Becket escorted him to hospital in Milan. "He was in the ward all day after the accident, and he was strapped up like a mummy. I thought it was time to go home, because Robert was going to be flown back to Ulster. There was another man who looked like a mummy also in the room, and eventually I said to Robert, 'I'll take your clothes home.' No sooner had I said this and made a move than the second 'mummy' looked as though he had taken a fit and tried to grab the clothes. I yelled for the nurse and told her the man seemed to be having problems. She didn't know what I meant and sent for an interpreter. The interpreter spoke to the man—the second mummy—and he informed the interpreter that I was trying to steal his whole wardrobe. I thought that his clothes were Robert's and he was making a vain attempt tot rescue them."

>> Robert Dunlop sits on the 250cc grid
at the North West 200 in 1986

>> A happy Robert Dunlop at the North West 200 in 1986 after scoring his first international road race win.

Beckett, who could fill a book with reminiscences about Robert, his lifelong pal, told me: "Having been brought up in the same town and following motorcycling, how could I not possibly link up with Robert Dunlop? I remember my uncle Jackie Graham, who was a mechanic for Joey, saying to me in those days—1986—that Joey was grabbing all the headlines; but Jackie was helping Robert as well. Jackie rang me and told me that Robert was working in an old shed. I had a garage at home and I offered to lend it to him. He had nobody. But he had great talent, although no self-belief. Patsy O'Kane, his sponsor for many years, tried to instill that belief in him, and they were close. But I always felt at the time that Robert lacked focus and was more outgoing than Joey.

"Let's put it this way: if Joey was racing and came in to refuel or make an adjustment to the bike he would do so with a fixed look on his face: nothing else mattered. However, if Robert came in he was quickly off the mark with some quips and classic comments, and I got the impression he wasn't really at that time paying attention to the job in hand.

>> Robert Dunlop is congratulated by his sponsor, P. J. O'Kane, after Robert was named Enkalon Irish Motorcyclist of the Year in 1987.

>> Robert Dunlop takes his first international road race win at the North West 200 in 1986. Pictured with him are Miss North West 200 and the runner-up, Gene McDonnell.

"I told him he was talented, and he certainly was. He got on so well with the people in the Far East that he wanted to go back to Macau every year. Our first was 1988, when Robert finished third. Kevin Swantz won the race and was so impressed with Robert that he wanted to meet the 'wee guy from Ireland.'

"Robert was racing a Honda with cattle-horn handlebars, which means they were turned upside down. This was P. J. O'Kane's RC30, and Robert gave a good exhibition, so much so that Swantz decided to have a drink with him that night after the race."

Apart from Liam Beckett and Dunlop's wife, Louise, the person who helped Robert along his way and made him into the man he became was a Londonderry haulier, Patsy O'Kane. Pasty met Robert in 1986 when Patsy was sponsoring the Londoner Gary Lingham on an RG Suzuki. O'Kane and Lingham parted company, and Lingham brought the bike from England around NW200 time.

>> Robert Dunlop (17, Suzuki) follows his brother Joey (3, Honda) with Alan Irwin close behind the pair of them during the 1987 Neil Robinson Memorial meeting at Kirkistown, Co. Down, in 1987.

Dunlop's uncle Robert Barkeley asked O'Kane to allow Robert to ride the big bike, and Louise and Robert both descended on O'Kane and tried to get him to give his consent.

O'Kane told me in later years: "I didn't want to give him the big bike, in case it rolled him. But eventually we agreed, and Robert went on to win the big race at the Tandragee 100.

"We became close friends after that and I helped to steer Robert through all sorts of problems. Probably the one that kept cropping up more than any other was the fact that Robert was prone to accidents. I paid all his surgery bills and operations on his hands. In many ways he was a substitute for the son I never had. For his part, Robert never forgot what I had done and the good days we had together, and every Christmas he brought a bunch a flowers and a card for my wife, Jean. We have no family, and we regarded Robert as one of our own."

Life was not always smooth between O'Kane and Dunlop, however, for Robert could sometimes be a bit wayward in looking to his immediate future. There was one occasion when O'Kane had bought him a Honda 125cc bike, but Robert was hoping to get one from the Honda factory. Needless to say, O'Kane wasn't too pleased. "I still miss him big-time, however," said Patsy. "I have many memories of him and remember the times

>> Robert Dunlop crashes in the 125cc race at Metropole in the North West 200 in 1989.

when he could be mild as a lamb and also strong as a lion. He was never in the same mood for very long and had various ways of getting round you. But no matter what happened, and often you might fall out with him, he had the lovable way of looking at you that made you want to put your arm around him and pat him on the head like a family pet.

"In my book he was one of the biggest riders Ireland ever produced, for he was able to win on the roads as well as circuits, and this put him one up on Joey.

"There are some who would say that Joey and Robert didn't get along, but this is nonsense. I remember one occasion—it was the night before the NW200—and Joey had problems starting the bike. The time was 3 a.m., and I told Robert that as Joey had Japanese mechanics over here helping him it was up to them to sort out Joey's problems. But Robert said to me, 'I think I've sussed out what's wrong with Joey's bike, and I'd like to tell him.' I asked why he would bother. Let him get on with it. But Robert wasn't happy, and I know he went to Joey and helped get his bike sorted out for the big race. That was the sort of him. He was always going to do a good turn if he could do so."

Robert Dunlop works on his brother Joey's RC45 Honda at the Ulster Grand Prix in 1999.

O'Kane's era with Dunlop was really the 1990s, but Robert before then had scored his first win on the roads at Fore, Co. Westmeath, in 1980, on a 50cc bike of all things. Robert's first Ulster win came on 7 August 1982, when he had a 125cc success on a Honda at the Mid-Antrim 150. This, in addition, was his first 125cc win anywhere.

Another man who was instrumental in helping the Robert Dunlop career roll along merrily was Willis Marshall, who was a keen fan of Robert's and wanted to become more actively involved. That opportunity came in 1997, when Robert was picking up the pieces from his big accident in 1994. He had made his return with his old friend and sponsor O'Kane in 1996, and this was well publicised when Robert and Patsy were told that they were not permitted to ride in that year's NW200.

Willis said: "I was involved as a journalist for the *Irish News,* and I decided to do an interview with Patsy on his association with Robert. I had followed with interest Robert's career from the late 80s, and I rated him as the best all-round rider that Ireland had ever produced. In many ways I regarded Robert as an even greater success than his brother, Joey.

Robert Dunlop with the converted bus that he used as a race transporter while racing for P. J. O'Kane.

>> Denis McCullough (2) leads the eventual race winner, Robert Dunlop (4), and Gary Dynes in the 125cc race at the Mid-Antrim road race meeting in 2000. Robert dedicated the win to his brother Joey who had been killed in Estonia just a few weeks earlier.

"While sitting with O'Kane I informed him that had Robert taken in three more short-circuit races in 1997 in the 125cc Superkings Championships and finished in the top five in each of those races he would have been the 1997 champion.

"Robert had finished in third place that year, and O'Kane was very interested, and when these facts were produced for him Patsy said, 'We never even knew that. If Robert or I had known that we would have taken more short circuits in that year.' It was there and then that O'Kane invited me to act as his team manager for 1998."

Robert and Patsy started their winning streak again in that year, but it was a confusing beginning. Robert had asked Patsy if he would buy him a new 125 Honda over the winter months of 1997, and Patsy, being a man of honour, did just that in the early months of 1998. Patsy had purchased a 1998 125, a bike that Robert described as the best he had ever ridden. Robert called with Patsy not long after O'Kane had purchased the Honda, and Patsy told Robert that he had the new bike for him.

>> Robert Dunlop on the O'Kane Honda at Ginger Hall during the 1998 Isle of Man TT.

"Robert seemed perplexed and told Patsy that he was trying to get a bike from Honda UK; but in the end Robert went with the O'Kane Honda for 1998—a combination that would prove very fruitful."

As Marshall says, the whole season was to be centred on the three big international road races: the NW200, the Isle of Man TT and the Ulster GP at Dundrod.

But Saturday 16 May would end with Robert in Coleraine Hospital after a very serious accident at the NW200. The 125cc race was stopped twice because of separate incidents on the opening laps, with the second incident at the Mill Road roundabout also

involving Robert. He was able to make it back to the pits minus a foot peg on the bike. As the other teams tended to their riders, with personnel wheeling out high-quality toolboxes, Liam Beckett produced a rusty old Rover biscuit tin, which Robert grabbed hold of and turned upside down, with the entire contents of rusty spanners, washers, nuts and bolts rolling all over the starting grid. In a flash Robert spied the tool he was looking for and started to take off the broken foot peg.

>> Robert Dunlop at work at the Ulster Grand Prix in 2007.

One of Dunlop's fellow-competitors, Alan Patterson, produced a replacement foot peg, and with seconds to spare the team started the race for a third time, but it would prove ill-fated. With the little 125cc machine safely off to a clean start, Robert was in the lead on the approach to Coleraine University when he appeared to be hit from behind by Davy Lemon.

He was flung into a telegraph pole, such was the force of the impact. It looked horrendous, and the race was stopped.

Marshall and O'Kane travelled down to Coleraine Hospital, where Robert was in a ward. Beckett had been by Robert's side the whole time. Robert had received a cracked bone in his right leg, broken collarbone, and concussion—injuries that would have kept most riders out of action for some time. Such was the impact of the crash that he bent a metal rod in his leg that had been inserted after his 1994 Isle of Man TT crash. The doctors at the time said that if it had not been for the pin in Robert's leg he would have received a very badly broken thigh bone. As far as the O'Kane racing team were concerned, the TT races in the Isle of Man were a non-starter.

>> Robert Dunlop on the O'Kane Honda at Quarterbridge during the 1998 Isle of Man TT.

>> Robert Dunlop receives physiotherapy from Fiona Gilliland at the TT in 1998.

"Robert was passed fit to race after faking that all was well, and he went to the Isle of Man. On the Wednesday night practice Robert set the fastest lap ever for a 125 machine, at 112 mph.

"Patsy and I arrived in the Isle of Man on the Monday of race week for the four-lap TT. Robert had employed the expert skills of the physiotherapist Fiona Gilliland, who had done wonders on Robert's leg and ankle. She was very much part of his success at that year's TT.

"With rain looming, the race was cut to three laps, with Robert blasting off down the Glen Crutchery Road like something expelled from the barrel of a gun. He was flying. At Glen Helen on lap 1 Robert had opened up a three-second lead, and the rest is history.

"It was a very emotional scene in the *parc fermé* as Robert was engulfed by well-wishers. I remember with a smile the Honda UK manager coming over and congratulating Robert and saying this was another win for Honda at the TT. Patsy was not long in moving in and said it was in fact a win for the O'Kane Honda—not the works job. The Honda man looked rather taken aback by this, but Patsy was right."

>> Robert Dunlop celebrates his Ultra-Lightweight TT win with third placeman, Owen McNally, at the 1998 Isle of Man TT.

Marshall later asked Robert how he got such a turn of speed from the bike, and Robert told an interesting story. He said that he and Beckett had found a new way to keep the race fuel cold. They had taken jerry-cans of fuel to a local butcher in Douglas at dead of night before the race and stored the fuel at 28 degrees Celsius. It was retrieved from the freezer an hour before the race and put into the bike. Apparently the fuel works at its peak at this temperature.

Robert's TT success in 1998 was argued as being the greatest feat of winning against the odds. In what other sport would you find such heroics? Robert continued his international winning ways in 1998 when he won at the Ulster GP and set up a new lap record.

What you saw with Robert was what you got. Marshall, who developed a close relationship with the rider, said: "I was sitting with him in the van at the Carrowdore 100 in 1998 when I noticed he had two different boots on prior to the race. His left boot zip had gone, and Robert had taken good use of a pair of scissors and a boot lace and threaded up his boot. So he had one boot with laces and the other with a zip. That same year I recall an old man asking Robert at the TT did he ever get nervous before a race. Robert's reply was worthy of repeating. He said, 'Just about as nervous as a cat with a long tail walking through a room full of rocking chairs.' Everyone was in stitches.

> Robert Dunlop was for me a giant of a man, even though he was small in stature.

"Robert Dunlop was for me a giant of a man, even though he was small in stature. No-one deserved an award more than Robert Dunlop. He never suffered fools gladly, but he was never one to hold a grudge."

Robert and Patsy parted company at the end of 1998, and Willis remembers meeting Robert on a dark November night in Newry when he took him to Co. Meath to meet his new sponsors, Crossan Motorcycles. There they met Adrian and Shane Fagan, and a deal was done over a bottle of beer. Robert was back on track.

Willis added: "The sport of motorcycling in Ireland just did not appreciate Robert Dunlop in the way that he deserved. No-one has come close to him, and no-one ever will."

>> Robert Dunlop leaps Ballaugh Bridge on his 125cc Crossan Honda on his way to third place in the Ultra-Lightweight TT in the Isle of Man in 2002.

Chapter 3

Battling
officialdom

>> Robert Dunlop in action on the O'Kane Honda during the Ultra-Lightweight TT at Bradden Bridge in 1997.

The year 1996 looked like being a big one for Dunlop. After his long spell in hospital he was now back in action, along with a thumb brake, which was unusual, to say the least, and caused some raised eyebrows in places. What it meant was that, as Robert couldn't use his right hand effectively to operate his brake, the brake grip was switched to the left-hand side of the machine and had a thumb control.

There were many who said that this brake was a bit precarious, for Dunlop was travelling at speeds of around 150 mph and it was pointed out by officialdom that his obvious inclination when braking would be to grab the right-hand side of the handlebars, and this was his bad hand.

So he had to get used to braking with his left hand as well as changing the clutch. He was in fact a left-handed rider.

However, this didn't matter to the public at large, most of whom were unaware of the changes to Dunlop's machine. These changes were soon to be made abundantly clear as the case of Robert Dunlop, his thumb grip and the NW200 soon became a *cause célèbre*.

One spring night in 1996, at about 10 p.m., I was greeted on my doorstep by Patsy O'Kane—one might say an ashen-faced O'Kane, for he told me that Robert Dunlop had been barred from taking part in the NW200. The reason given by Billy Nutt, clerk of the course at the time, was that he felt Dunlop was liable to affect the safety not only of himself but of other riders.

Patsy sat in my conservatory and recounted the whole story. He was lost for words. After all, Dunlop had already raced that year in the Tandragee 100, and it seemed ridiculous that he would be barred from taking part in his home road race. "I'm not going to let this rest," said an ebullient Patsy. "I'll take legal action if necessary."

And this was what he did. Most of the early part of 1996 saw Robert Dunlop, Patsy O'Kane and the Motorcycle Union of Ireland, including Billy Nutt, swamped in litigation before the whole matter was sorted out in time for the Ulster GP in August.

Years later Nutt told me how the whole saga of the NW200 came about. After all, Robert was a big name—one of the biggest names in the North West. As my colleague Harold Crooks recounted, "I went into a shop in Ballymena and was assailed by a shop assistant who said to me, 'What are you doing to wee Robert Dunlop? Why isn't he allowed to ride at the NW200?' Harold was the race commentator at the time, and he felt personally involved.

>> Joey and Robert Dunlop share some body language as they pull on their race gloves on the grid at the North West 200 in 1990.

However, let's tune in to Billy Nutt. He gave me the view held by the promoters of the big race. "Robert used to live in those days on the Randalstown–Portglenone–Belfast Road. I would often call in to him to see how he was getting on. He seemed to be progressing, but shortly before the NW200 I was sitting having tea with him when I noticed that he had a plate on his knee which he had difficultly manoeuvring.

"The situation was that he had to move his fork to his left hand in order to cut what was in front of him. People who aren't injured would naturally use the right hand. Robert would transfer the knife back to the right hand and continue to eat. I thought this was somewhat worrying as to his health, and I thought that with over thirty riders in opposition against him at the North West at speeds of around 130 mph Robert might have difficultly keeping up with the pace, especially as he didn't have the use of that right hand. I felt he just couldn't handle the bike properly.

Robert Dunlop's 125cc machine in 1997 showing clearly there is no front brake on the right hand side of the bike. The brake lever, operated by Robert's thumb, had been moved to the left hand side beside the clutch lever following the injuries he sustained in 1994.

>> Robert Dunlop,
the most successful
North West 200 rider in history,
sits on the grid at the start of
practice for the
2007 event.

"I was certainly concerned, and one morning I woke up at 6:30 a.m. with this on my mind. I quickly made my mind up and I told the race secretary, Mervyn Whyte, not to send Robert any entries for the race. I went off that afternoon to inform Robert that he wasn't going to be allowed to ride. Louise was there, and the pair of them perhaps were relieved the decision had been made.

Robert Dunlop (Norton) reads his pit board held by Davy Wood who has stepped out on to the track to display it at the North West 200 in 1990.

"Other people thought differently, but this was an honest gesture on my part. Still, we got a lot of stick about it, and appeals to the Motorcycle Union of Ireland to allow Robert to ride fell like snowflakes.

"There was even another and sinister element about the protest, for a few hours before the race some so-called fans had put nails on the track. Marshals soon cleared them up, the police were excellent; there were no mishaps or race delays. Still, I always remember that incident and what might have happened had the race been allowed to go on."

This was not the only NW200 incident involving Dunlop. He seemed to thrive on them. The following year, while practising for the race at Ballykelly Airfield he fell off and injured that famous right arm. He was immediately taken to Altnagelvin Hospital in Co. Londonderry and stayed there for a few days before moving back to his old sanctuary, the Ulster Hospital in Dundonald.

Liam Beckett, who, needless to say, was at Ballykelly for yet another crash saga, said: "The bike seized after I had run the machine in. There are no bends at Ballykelly, as you know: it was straight up and down. I was standing at the end of the runway when Robert crashed, and it was a case of 'off to hospital again'."

Beckett also made the point that the fact that Robert had difficulty with small objects did not mean that he couldn't race or handle a bike, as was pointed out in some quarters. "There was a Dr Stephens in the Isle of Man who said that small objects created a problem in these cases, and while Robert felt he was handling things properly in effect this wasn't the case at all."

Beckett was a tower of strength to Robert, and especially so when it came to battling with officialdom.

>> Robert Dunlop dicing with Alan Patterson in the 125cc race at the 1990 North West 200.

That year of 1997, when he fell off at Ballykelly, followed the drama of midsummer 1996 when, apart from the NW200 ban, Dunlop was almost refused permission to race at the Dundrod 150. Jim Cray, who was steward at the meeting in June, said: "I wasn't happy about that thumb brake, and a lot of people agreed with me. We had a stewards' meeting and we decided that we shouldn't let Robert race at that meeting. However, the clerk of the course, Davy Rea, put himself in the line of fire when he said that in his view Robert could race, and that was his decision. He more or less said that the stewards' view would take second place to his. We alerted Davy to the situation he was in and pointed out that if anything happened to Robert in the race Davy would be held responsible. As it turned out, Robert was allowed to race, and believe it or not he won the 125cc race—thumb brake and all. It was an amazing time; but there was more to follow.

>> Robert Dunlop in action on the O'Kane Honda during
the Ultra-Lightweight TT at Bradden Bridge in 1997.

85

>> Close to the action! The marshals get a close-up view of the battle for second place at Tournagrough as Gary Dynes leads Robert Dunlop and Denis McCullough in the 125cc race at the Dundrod 150 meeting in 2000.

>> Robert Dunlop in action on the 125cc O'Kane Honda at the 1998 North West 200.

"With all the appeals and counter-appeals, one was inclined to get dizzy. Robert had now taken legal action, along with Patsy O'Kane, and Patsy's solicitor was now looking after the case. In 1996, the year of the win in the Dundrod 150, Dunlop appealed against the fact that we had decided not to issue him with an international licence. This meant he would not be allowed to ride at the Ulster GP.

"So off we trooped down to Dundrod for an intercentre appeal meeting on Robert Dunlop. Robert's solicitor, Seán Doherty, was there, along with Patsy, and it was obvious they meant business. At one stage the president of the Motorcycle Union of Ireland, Frank Semple, walked out and someone else took over the role. Frank felt he should have chaired the committee of appeal.

>> Robert Dunlop in action at Castle Corner in the 125cc race at the
1999 Tandragee 100.

"More problems followed when the chain of office went astray after it was handed back to the union. In fact during my year of office, in 2000, it was still missing.

"All had now, however, been returned to normality, and the Dunlop case—the 'will he or won't he' over the international licence—and the other problems were soon resolved. But I can tell you it was a hectic time for the officials concerned, and I'm also sure it was something which Robert himself didn't want, although to be honest he seemed to be surrounded by controversy."

"One of Dunlop's closest friends in road racing was the urbane Barry Symmons, an Englishman who has made his home in Belfast. I first met Symmons in 1978 when he was manager of the Honda team, which included the headliner Phil Read. Read had failed to turn up for the Ulster GP that year, and I remember asking Symmons, who I didn't know, what was going to happen. Would Read be here for the practice? Symmons, however, stared me out and more or less intimated that all would be well and that I was making a big fuss about nothing. As someone said to me afterwards, 'Barry is always the firm's man.'

"Well, as it turned out, this was not a happy ending as far as Symmons and the rest of us were concerned, for Read turned up on race day, having missed practice, and after a meeting with the clerk of the course, Kevin Martin, it was decided that he could not take part. Kevin was amazing and was as tough and intuitive as they come. Could you imagine a big name like Read being barred nowadays?

"Anyway, back to Dunlop, and we have two to consider. Joey was the first man to be taken under Symmons's wing when he was manager of Honda, and during the years that he won the five World Formula 1 Championships Joey was always guided by Barry. They toured the world together, and Symmons became a highly respected and effective figure. He signed Joey for Honda in 1980, and coincidentally he signed Robert for Norton in 1990.

>> Robert Dunlop leads Ian Lougher and his brother Joey in the 250cc race at Church Corner during the 1991 North West 200.

>> Robert Dunlop in action on the Norton at the 1991 North West 200.

>> Joey and Robert Dunlop chat at the Isle of Man TT prizegiving in the Villa Marina in 2000.

How this came about is quite simple. Symmons had been headhunted by Norton, and they were obviously looking for a top rider. Symmons told me: "I remember first meeting Robert when we were looking after Joey. I went to Robert and Joey's house and watched Joey and Robert ride up and down outside. This was common practice in those days at the little village which was the fulcrum of the Armoy Armada. Joey was working on a new 125cc Honda and he told me about Robert. Joey said, 'He's good. You'd better believe it. He might even beat me and give me a hard time.'"

At that time Honda needed someone in the Isle of Man to ride a 250cc production bike in a one-off. Symmons had seen Robert ride at various meetings and he had shown great ability. As Symmons explained to me shortly after Robert's untimely death, "I think he was greater than Joey. What he did was come to terms with short-circuit racing when he won the British Championship in 1991. Joey also rode at times in the British title race, but he was never able to get on top of things in this sphere—in fact Joey for us was simply there for the TT. Robert was a different kettle of fish, and I believe he could have gone on to be World GP Champion. I signed him for Norton in 1990. At that time Norton had Steve Spray and Trevor Nation. Robert came in and wasn't immediately a success, for in his very first ride for us—a test at Snetterton on a damp day—would you believe that he crashed again. He highsided, broke his collarbone, and we took him

Robert Dunlop follows brother Joey around Ballyboley Corner in the 125cc race at the Carrowdore 100 in 1993.

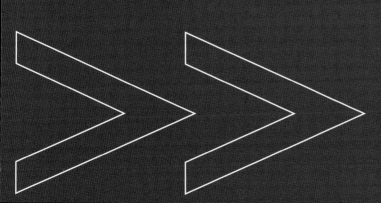

to the accident and emergency part of Norwich Hospital. In fact he was seeing more of the inside of hospitals than he was of winners' enclosures. Robert, however, said to us not to worry and that he wouldn't let the Norton get the better of him again, and he never did.

>> **Robert Dunlop on the Norton at Metropole during the Superbike race at the 1991 North West 200.**

"Robert was an amazing sight clinging to the big Norton, and for a number of years he was a spectacular addition to all race programmes. He won the NW200 for us in 1990, when he had a double, and he went from strength to strength after that. His secret was his complete control of nerves. Some competitors override, but Robert preferred a laid-back attitude, which showed him to be an intelligent rider as well as one who was very brave. As I have said earlier, I thought he would have been a world champion, which I pointed out at the Old Bailey when Robert was suing the Medd people after his accident at the 1994 Isle of Man TT.

Robert Dunlop celebrates a win at the North West 200 in 1990.

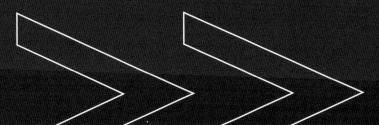
>> Sibling rivalry! Joey Dunlop and his younger brother Robert do battle in the 125cc race at the Enkalon Trophy meeting at Aghadowey, Co. Londonderry, at the start of the Irish road racing season in 2000.

>> Robert Dunlop with his dogs.

"I said that at that time he was on the threshold of the World GP scene with the 125cc bike, and I still feel that this is true. I remember in the British GP at Donington when he was a wild card he was told to make his bike heavier. So he and Liam Beckett got a G clamp, which did the job. Incredible as it may seem, this clamp—which he had no intention of racing with—stuck out at 90 degrees, and in many ways it was a bit of a joke on the part of Dunlop and Beckett, who were always up to some mischief. As it turned out, the scrutineers unbelievably decided to come around the outside of the bike and missed the G clamp. Everybody was amazed, and of course Robert didn't use the clamp in the race; but it just shows you what can happen.

"The following week at Assen there were more Dunlop problems with weight. The bike was excluded after the race for being too light, and Robert quipped, 'I must have left the G clamp in my other leathers.'"

>> Robert Dunlop receives the Lifetime Achievement award from Steve Parrish at the Irish Racer Irish Motorcyclist of the Year awards in Belfast in 2005.

Symmons, when talking about the Old Bailey trial, said: "I told everyone in court that his horrific Isle of Man accident had wrecked his career completely. Steve Parrish and Roger Burnett, who were for the insurers, said that Dunlop's compensation should be worth y. I said that it should be worth x. The judge decided somewhere in between, but I know Robert was quite happy in court with what he had been awarded."

There have always been arguments among us about who was the better, Joey or Robert.

Barry Symmons has given his view impartially, but at the end of the day it comes down to opinion. The battle of the brothers at the Ulster GP in 1990 in many ways silenced a lot of sceptics, who said that Joey was finished after his big accident at Brands Hatch in 1989.

Robert was on the Norton and Joey on the Honda in the race of aces, as it was later called. With the new World Superbike Championship rapidly gaining momentum, from 1990 the Formula 1 title would no longer hold full world champion status and survived as the FIM Cup. The five-round campaign arrived at Dundrod in August 1990 via Japan, the Isle of Man, Portugal and Finland, with Steven Hislop as firm pre-race favourite.

>> Joey Dunlop (Honda) chases his brother Robert (Norton) around Metropole during the Superbike race at the 1991 North West 200.

But less than a lap into the thirteen-lap race Hislop was touring. His challenge ended with a jammed gear change. He went into his pit and set off on a futile ride that would eventually end in sixteenth place. But the headline would proclaim another historic chapter of the story of the Dunlop brothers, although at that time most of the focus was on Joey. The race ended, to the delight of the thousands who lined Dundrod, with Joey crossing the line, clenched fist in the air, with nineteen seconds to spare.

It all revolved around a pit stop. In those days a rider was likely to have to make a refuel at some stage, because of the length of the race, and, needless to say, everyone expected Joey and Robert to do the same. As it turned out, however, while Robert made his pit stop on the Norton, Joey blasted through on the Honda, to the intense excitement of the packed stands.

In 2003 Robert recalled the epic race. He said: "Joey was a bit emotional about that one. I did the world championship and raced the Norton at places like Portugal and Finland. The Norton was very fast, which suited parts of Dundrod, and parts it didn't suit. Dundrod is a very all-round circuit. You can be a fast rider and not win there.

> Road racing is hard to perfect, but Joey had it down to a fine art.

"I got on in front by quite a bit in that race. I could see it was Joey behind, but he was so far back I thought I would keep on riding the way I was doing, which was fast and safe enough. After a couple of laps I had a look back again. I could see he was getting closer. I thought, I better kick on a bit, and I remember having a look at Leathemstown and then again before Ireland's Corner, and the gap was pretty much the same. By then I started to ride harder and was going as fast as I could go. He passed me at the Windmill. It's a fast section, and my bike was fast, but still he managed it.

"Road racing is hard to perfect, but Joey had it down to a fine art. He just pulled so much ground on me from Ireland's to Wheelers. So I thought, I can't have this. I passed him again going into the hairpin and stayed in front until the end of the lap, when I had to come in to refuel. I didn't know he could do the distance without refuelling, and I'm sure I could have held him on the straight, because my bike was faster than his, but he would probably have passed me by the time we got to Budore.

"I always admired Joey for that one. People said to me afterwards I would have beaten him if I hadn't had to refuel, but I don't honestly believe I would."

Joey Dunlop receives the winner's trophy after winning the Ulster Grand Prix TT Formula One race at Dundrod in 1990. Joey beat his brother Robert to win his first big bike race since his horrific crash at Brands Hatch in 1989.

Chapter 4 >> >>

The sinking of the *Tornamona*

Robert Dunlop in action on the O'Kane RC30 Honda in the 1988 Formula One TT in the Isle of Man.
Photograph by David Collister.

Throughout his amazingly theatrical career, Robert Dunlop was the master of the quick quip. When I was stuck for a story I used to ring Robert and ask him about what his plans were, and without fail he would not only elucidate those plans but would gave me a phrase that I could use in my article. I don't know this for certain but I gathered that Robert did a lot of reading, and that being so, he was never stuck for words.

At the paddock before a motorcycle meeting Robert used to strut about and chat about his prospects. He would also leave me with something to hang the story on. He never liked to disappoint reporters, and it's a true saying that if there was a story in motorcycling the first thing the broadcasting companies would do would be to call for Robert.

>> The cameras were never far away from Robert Dunlop in a race paddock.

An early racing picture of Robert Dunlop on a 125cc machine at Aghadowey, Co. Londonderry.

The North West 200's most successful racers, Michael Rutter and Robert Dunlop, on a windswept

His ability to sum things up at the drop of a hat and make others laugh was never more in evidence and was certainly badly needed on the occasion when the fishing-boat on which he was travelling with Joey to the Isle of Man sank after striking rocks at the entrance to Strangford Lough in Co. Down.

It was a night when Robert and Joey, along with ten others, nearly lost their lives, and the story was told throughout the country. It all happened when Joey and Robert and the others decided to make their annual pilgrimage to the Isle of Man on the fishing-boat *Tornamona*. This was a superstitious act of faith as far as Joey was concerned, for he had travelled on this boat to the Isle of Man in 1980, when he scored his first major success at the TT—the Classic Race, which in those days was for the fastest machines at the meeting. This was Joey's breakthrough, and he reckoned that if the boat was lucky for him in 1980 it would be lucky for him for ever more. That's the way he looked at it.

But it was all to go horribly wrong, and only Robert Dunlop's sense of humour and his quick wits prevented morale from sinking along with the boat.

>> Robert Dunlop gives the Rev. Ian Paisley a push start on his 125cc Honda during a visit by the local MP to Robert's Ballymoney home to wish the rider well in the forthcoming North West 200 in 2003.

The boat was moving out of Strangford Lough when it had to turn round to Portaferry at the head of the Lough and pick up a bike that had been left behind. The *Tornamona* was packed with machines ready for the Isle of Man, strapped down on the decks accordingly. However, the decision to turn back and pick up the missing bike had horrible consequences, for the boat missed the tide on the way back up the Lough, ran into rough water, smashed into the rocks, and was on the way to sinking.

The story is told that Joey and Robert were cooking a fry for the rest of the boys, and in a later interview Robert said, "I was frying two sausages and I was asked was there any salt." Before long there was enough salt to fill a ship, as the sea water burst through and the *Tornamona* began to sink.

>> Robert Dunlop leads Darran Lindsay and Chris Palmer through Church Bends during their titanic tussle in the 125cc race at the Southern 100 in the Isle of Man in 2006. Robert won by 1/100th of a second.

>> Robert Dunlop pulls on his boots ready for action at the Isle of Man TT in 2000.

>> Robert Dunlop flies over Ballaugh Bridge on his way to fastest 125cc lap time during Thursday afternoon practice at the Isle of Man TT in 2002.

<< Robert Dunlop (125cc Honda) in action at Creg ny Baa during the Ultra-Lightweight TT in the Isle of Man in 2003.

What happened afterwards was a fight for life on the part of those on board. To be fair, there was no panic, except for one passenger who was so afraid of the water that he refused to go into a dinghy and had to be coaxed off the boat.

Robert and Joey played their part like heroes, and they took charge of unstrapping all the bikes that had been tied to the deck. This took some considerable time, but eventually the job was done, and Robert and Joey threw jerry-cans out onto the heaving sea in order to have something to cling to. It was midnight and pitch-black. How no-one was drowned remains a mystery, but everything turned out happily, and both Dunlops were eventually able to go to the TT.

>> Robert and Joey Dunlop in the Isle of Man TT winners' enclosure in 2000 after Joey won the Ultra-Lightweight TT and Robert was third. It was Joey's last TT win and the last time the brothers raced against each other.

Meanwhile at Robert's home, Louise wasn't aware of the drama taking place on Strangford Lough. The first she heard of it was when Robert's mother, May, came to the door to say she had heard there had been an accident involving the brothers on Strangford Lough. Louise said: "She sat with us until we got further news. We didn't realise that the boat had capsized, and we had no idea that Robert and Joey were in the water. They were both bad sailors. I thought that they would probably throw the bikes overboard and survive without going down. It was only later that I learnt that everyone had ended up in the water and that they had a fight on their hands making shore.

>> Robert Dunlop rides one of Louise's horses at his Ballymoney home in 2001.

"There were no mobile phones in those days, and eventually we got a phone call that everyone was safe. Robert rang to say he was all right but very cold, wet, and shocked."

He also added he was annoyed that he had lost everything: his bikes, his kit—the lot; and all had to be salvaged as soon as possible. He still intended to ride in the TT, despite what had happened. "He told me it was a really scaring time—the worst in his life—for he added he did not like the water. He told me there was white foam everywhere as the waves surged around the ship, and he had no life jacket, but the dinghies came to the rescue and all the passengers were able to clamber on board. The bikes had been cut free, but this added another problem, for obviously they had to be 'rescued' in their own right.

> You know, Robert said at the time he thought he might die that night.

"You know, Robert said at the time he thought he might die that night. He said he had never met anything like it, and there was a problem when one of the party, Andy English, made it clear that he couldn't swim. Robert said he had tried to calm everyone down—and bear in mind that he was only twenty-three years old at the time."

>> Robert Dunlop in the 1980s.

<< Robert Dunlop (Crossan Honda) negotiates Guthries Bends during TT practice in 2002.

The reason for the drama of the *Tornamona* was soon made clear. After the boat had set sail for the Isle of Man a call came through requesting it to turn around and pick up a bike belonging to another TT competitor, Brian Reid. It was this omission that caused all the problems and that nearly led to disaster.

Before the boat sank, all the men on board were in good spirits, and Joey fancied his chances for a treble—which he later accomplished at that year's TT races. In 1985 he was world champion and was going for broke.

But back to Portaferry and the beginning of the drama. A lorry had driven up to the quayside, and on it was Brian Reid's bike. The call was to bring the boat back again to pick up the machine. The skipper answered the message, and they all agreed they should return. It was a disastrous move.

On board, Joey and Robert had dozed off when they were awakened by a large crash. Then the lights went out. They got up and looked over the side and saw that the boat had struck the rocks. They managed to free the dinghies and were just clear of the boat when it sank.

Portaferry lifeboat was launched immediately, but because of the rough seas a stronger offshore vessel from Donaghadee—a type similar to that which saved passengers from the ill-fated *Princess Victoria* in the North Channel in 1953—was called out as back-up. Coastguard rescue parties from nearby Ardglass and Portaferry were also mobilised, and an RAF helicopter equipped with a high-intensity searchlight was called in from Aldergrove, near Belfast Airport. Twenty-one minutes after the original mayday call the skipper of the *Tornamona* radioed the coastguard again to tell rescuers that water had reached its batteries and that they were losing communication. They eventually abandoned ship and fired flares to draw attention to themselves.

Some thirty-seven minutes after the drama began, Portaferry lifeboat pinpointed the rafts and took them in towards shore. The men were then transferred to a larger boat that was helping with the rescue operation, and all were landed safely in Portaferry at 1:23 a.m.

By this time the *Tornamona*, with its precious cargo of racing motorcycles and expensive parts, had disappeared, leaving Joey and Robert Dunlop and their pals gazing forlornly at the murky depths. How were these bikes to be recovered?

≪ Robert Dunlop (125cc Honda) in action at Handley's Bend during the Ultra-Lightweight TT practice in the Isle of Man in 2003.

> Celebrating the 25th anniversary of the Enkalon Irish Motorcyclist of the Year awards in 2004 are past winners Con Law, Darran Lindsay, Adrian Coates, Derek Young, Robert Dunlop and Brian Reid (on bike).

Brian Reid recalled the tale to me. "My memory is that the Cookstown 100 road race took place on the Saturday, but the normal ferry for the Isle of Man left on the Friday, so if you wanted to go to Cookstown you couldn't get the ferry from Belfast. We had organised to do the Cookstown with one bike and then send it along with Joey's team on the boat to the Isle of Man.

"Joey's own bikes had already gone to the Island. We went to the Cookstown race and it poured. I felt as if I was getting the flu, and as the bike was brand-new I thought I would rather not go out on it on a dirty day, not feeling well. I decided to pack up and return home early and get ready to go to the Isle of Man, so I didn't race that day at all

"Billy McKinstry, an auto electrician who was sponsoring Sam McClements, said he would take my bike down to the boat along with Sam's and collect it later that evening. All the rest of my bikes were in the Isle of Man. They had gone on the ferry on the Friday. Because I wasn't feeling well, Billy said he would take my bike down with the other bike belonging to McClements. Dunlop and the boys had told me that the bike had to be at Portaferry at 11 p.m. that night, as that was when they were leaving. So McKinstry arrived at my home in Dromore, Co. Down, to pick up my bike, and he wasn't in any particular hurry, as it was a long way off 11 p.m. We loaded the bike up and had a bit of a chat, and as far as I was concerned that was the end of it.

"Then at about three or four o'clock in the morning I was woken out of my sleep by another rider, Noel Hudson, who had rung to say that the boat had sunk. I thought, 'Boat? What boat? What are you talking about?' So he gave me the number of the local police station in Portaferry. I rang them and they said that the boat had sunk and all the bikes were down, but that everybody had been rescued.

"What had actually happened was that Billy had driven to Portaferry with the two bikes, and when he got there the boat had gone, so he was about to turn and come back again when somebody in a boat shouted up, 'Are you looking for the fishing boat?' Billy said he was, so the person in the boat said, 'Well, they've just left about ten minutes ago. Do you want me to radio them and ask them to come back?' Billy said that would be a great help. So they radioed the fishing boat. The *Tornamona* turned around and came back, and they loaded the two bikes onto the boat. Seemingly they wasted so much time doing this that they missed the tide, and when they went back out again the tide was against them. Instead of going forward they ran sideways and ran onto the rocks.

Needless to say, I never slept the rest of the night after that phone call.

"Needless to say, I never slept the rest of the night after that phone call, and as soon as it came to eight o'clock I was on the phone, ringing round several people to try and organise divers. The divers were keen to get going, just to see the bikes and get them up. As soon as I arrived in Portaferry all these men were there ready to help me get my bike.

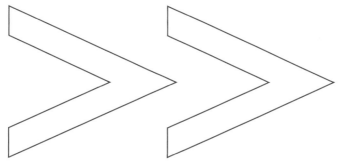

124

"They were diving all day, and I stood there watching bikes come up. I became more despondent, for none of them was mine. It was getting frustrating. Eventually they had to leave it, and it was the following day before the bike was raised to the surface."

Meanwhile Robert Dunlop also had his bike rescued, but in those days he wasn't really the star he later became. Everyone was interested in Joey, and the fact that Robert was competing as well was almost incidental.

But the two boys were something else, as they say. Joey and Robert had a unique personality. They were totally focused on what they were doing, and it would have taken something like an earthquake or other natural disaster to prevent the Dunlops taking part in a road race.

As Louise Dunlop said in later years, "Robert would have gone anywhere to race. I remember one time he was riding in the World Superbike Championship and he went ahead in a series in which he had no knowledge. He said he would give it a go, and you know, over all the years he never seemed to get any slower."

The inimitable Liam Beckett recalled: "I wasn't with Robert in those days. It was 'before my time.' But I remember Robert telling me that the whole Strangford Lough drama was a nerve-racking experience. At the same time he took it all in his stride. When you think about it, a fishing boat sinking in rough seas means nothing to a rider who competes at places like the Isle of Man. These riders believe they lead a charmed life, and this was certainly the case where Robert was concerned. He always seemed to bounce back and had incredible will to compete. I don't think there has been anything like him in Ulster sport."

>> Robert Dunlop keeps watch at the Co. Down coast in 1985 as he waits to hear news of the stricken fishing boat that had sank the day before whilst carrying his and his brother Joey's bikes to the Isle of Man TT.

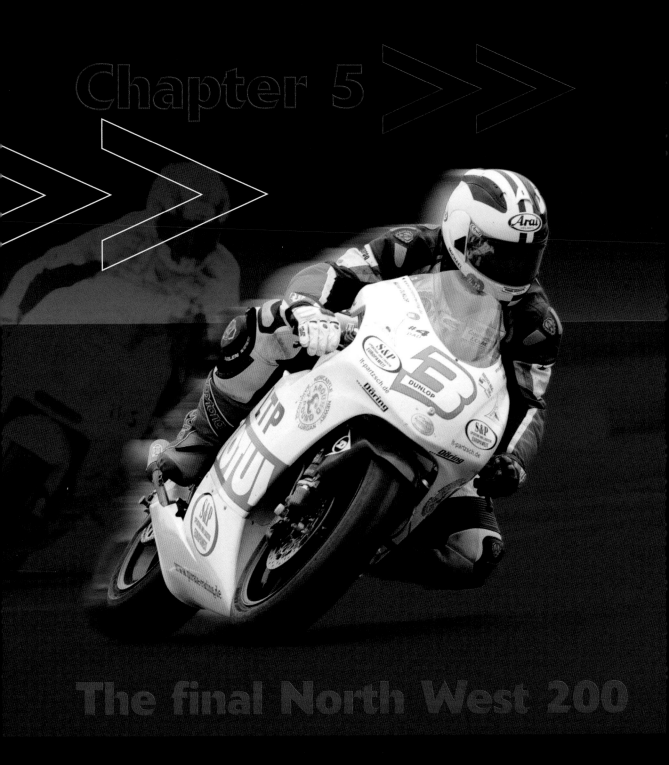

Chapter 5

The final North West 200

>> Michael Dunlop on his way to winning the 250cc race at the North West 200 in 2008.

"The Robert Dunlop death hit me for six. I will never forget it, and in many ways it put blight on the North West 200." This was the stark view of Mervyn Whyte, clerk of the course who was on duty on the evening of 15 May 2008 when Dunlop crashed at Mathers Cross. "I was on the scene within two minutes, and Robert was still alive. But, tragically, he died on the way to hospital.

In my time at the head of this race from 2001 I had no fatalities to be concerned about. I began to get a little complacent, but Dunlop's death had its effect, not only on me but on everyone else. When this sort of thing happens you have to sit back and take stock. It was particularly unhappy, as the rider involved was Robert, who had given excellent support to the race over the years.

"After Robert's death I went to the hospital and then to Robert's home, where I spent a couple of hours with Louise, who informed me that the race should go on. She said, 'That would have been Robert's wishes.'

"Robert's sons William and Michael were in a state of shock. They found it hard to take in, and I could understand this. Then the story moved on and had an outcome which no-one could have predicted. On the Friday I had heard that William Dunlop had planned to race. At that stage it's fair to say I had certain reservations about the state of his mind, for he had been without a lot

>> Bikers leave flowers at the crash scene where race legend Robert Dunlop died at the North West 200 in May 2008.

of sleep during the dramatic period of his father's death. William rang me Friday afternoon and informed me he wanted to ride. He said he was fine and there was nothing to worry about. I told him that he should see me first thing on Saturday morning. He did see me and I talked to him. I was happy about him and thought everything would be all right. William is a tough competitor, and he certainly is no fool.

> Robert Dunlop, the most successful North West 200 rider in history, in action during practice for the 2007 event.

>> William Dunlop leads his father, Robert, and Ian Lougher during the 125cc race at Kells in 2003.

"Meanwhile the stewards had met and wouldn't allow William to ride. I was informed of this decision, and I must say I was quite happy.

"Then there was another twist to the story, for on Saturday morning—race day—I had a call from Michael Dunlop, who said he was stuck in traffic at the Lodge roundabout in Coleraine, which is near the course. Michael wanted to race as well. I kept the stewards informed, and they met again to say that neither William nor Michael should race.

>> Robert Dunlop cleans the visor of his son Michael's helmet before the start of the Pacemaker Press International 250cc race at the Ulster Grand Prix in 2007.

"When the roads were closed for the race I went on a final lap to see the roads were clear. On the car radio I received a call that, incredibly, both William and Michael were on the starting line. I told whoever phoned me to get the stewards in. I came back and saw the Dunlop boys on the grid. The stewards had an impromptu meeting at the side at the road and agreed they would have to let them ride. My view was it would have been difficult to take them off the grid. The place was full of photographers and press men, for the starting area at the NW200 is one of the busiest places in sport.

"What would have been the result of pictures showing the two Dunlops, forty-eight hours after their father's death, being dragged off the grid? It's just horrific to think of. So I thought it was in the best interests of everyone that they raced, but nobody could have envisaged that the result of this 250cc race—the first on the card—would end up with such a result. You couldn't haven't dreamed it up.

>> Michael Dunlop is comforted on the podium by his girlfriend, Jill, after winning the 250cc race at the North West 200 in 2008, just two days after his father, Robert, was killed during practice for the same race.

"Michael won the race—a class which his father had been intending to contest and in which his father had died during practice. And I can tell you that my feelings were virtually indescribable. I was in a total state of anxiety throughout the contest, and I was praying that nothing would happen to Michael. Fortunately, Michael came home safely, with the added bonus that he had won."

Meanwhile William was unfortunate in that he didn't get very far from the start, for his bike broke down. The triumph of Michael, however, did the race a favour, for it took the minds of all those thousands off the death of Robert Dunlop.

>> Michael Dunlop celebrates after winning the 250cc race at the North West 200 in 2008.

>> Robert Dunlop in action on the 125cc Honda during the opening practice session for the
North West 200 in 2008.

>> Robert Dunlop with his sons Michael and William at the North West 200 in 2006.

Robert would have wanted it no other way. He had coached his two sons and had given them his all.

William told me afterwards: "I owe everything to my dad. He was always there to fix the bike and to give me the right sort of advice when it came to competing. At first I wasn't going to race, but then I changed my mind, for I just threw myself into looking after my machine and making sure it was going to be ready for the Saturday."

Louise said: "William just blocked it off. He didn't want to talk about his father's death, and to be honest our house on the day after Robert's crash had a surreal feeling. Michael was handling the funeral arrangements, and William was stuck in the garage looking after his bike. He was helped by his fiancée, Caroline, and I suppose in this respect he was lucky to have some solace."

William's description of the accident that killed Robert is poignant. "I saw smoke coming out of the back of my dad's bike. I tried to pass him to warn him, but he was too quick for me. I stopped at Coleraine and heard there had been a crash. I thought, is it my dad or Michael?

"At first the crash didn't appear to be life-threatening, but I had a feeling in my bones that my dad would not make it. You may say it was a premonition if you wish; and the worst was confirmed when I hitched a lift to the Causeway Hospital and found out what happened to my dad. I can't tell you how I was feeling. It was dreadful."

I saw smoke coming out of the back of my dad's bike.
I tried to pass him to warn him, but he was too quick for me.

Michael Dunlop is a rotund character who is about twice the size of his father, but he gives the impression that he is very much a part of this Dunlop dynasty. While William appears to be more sensitive to all that's around him, Michael is the sort who doesn't let anything get in his way and pushes on, full bore.

> William Dunlop with his father, Robert, as they walk through the pits at the Clubman's event at Nutt's Corner in April 2001. This was one of William's first race meetings.

This was never more in evidence than when he decided to race at the virtual last minute—to be more precise the last two minutes—at the opening race at the North West.

With the death of his father felt by everyone around the circuit, no-one expected Michael to race, but that's just what he did. Michael told me: "I didn't know what to do. My father's body was lying in my house, and the funeral was very much on everyone's mind. With two minutes to go I made the decision to race. I know it sounds a little cold-blooded, but I had to get going again and put everything out of my mind. My 250cc bike was ready and had been set up by the German team whom I rode for. The bike was lying in the lorry, and Norman Rank, one of my two sponsors, was in a position to back me if I decided to race.

"Just before the practice lap took place I had some personal thoughts, which I don't want to divulge. But I felt my father's presence and I knew I'd win. It was something I couldn't express. I wasn't going to be beaten; but this wasn't just a case of trying hard to do well.

Michael Dunlop pictured with the special 'Dad no. 4' decal he wore on his bike when racing in the 250cc race at the North West 200 in 2008.

>> Robert Dunlop on the grid for the final time at the North West 200 in 2008.

This was an inspiration—I know of no other word—which prompted me onto that starting line. I know some people were surprised and a bit aghast that I was ready to race only days after my dad's death, but I felt this was what he would have wanted.

"The race itself, I was dicing with Christian Elkin, and I can tell you he didn't want to win as much as I did. I had planned what to do late in the race if everything went right—you know we Dunlops have a plan B whenever it's needed! To sum it up, I was going to win if my bike stayed in the race.

"After I received the chequered flag I was overwhelmed with congratulations. I had won the race in the most dramatic circumstances. Needless to say I was overjoyed, but I was conscious of the fact that I wasn't going to stay at the race meeting all day. I just packed it in and went straight home. I felt that was the place to be."

Robert Dunlop o
Hanna Honda in

<< A biker pays his respects at Robert Dunlop's funeral.

>> The huge crowd that congregated outside Garryduff Presbyterian Church for Robert Dunlop's funeral.

Meanwhile Louise gives her account of what happened on that dramatic day. "I didn't see anything live. I watched the race later. Before the start Jim Dunlop, Robert's brother, kept me informed by mobile phone of what was happening and whether Michael was going to race or not race.

<< The huge screen at the North West 200 paddock displayed images of Robert Dunlop throughout the day, following his fatal crash during the previous evening's practice session. All events were cancelled in the paddock area as a mark of respect.

"Bear in mind that Robert's body was still in our house, but I didn't want to stop Michael taking part, or William either. I was secretly relieved when initially the stewards didn't allow them to start; but when they did get the go-ahead I just thought, 'Whatever will be will be.'

"I was still getting over the shock of Robert's death after the meeting, but I must say Michael's win came just at the right time. It's just what Robert would have wanted."

Meanwhile Michael went on to the TT, and again there was much agonising before he took part. In fact he went from winning the 250cc at the North West to burying his father and then returning from the Isle of Man as the fastest of the six Dunlop family members to have raced at the course.

His best performance was a tenth place in the senior race, while William didn't go at all and preferred to ride in English short circuits.

> I was still getting over the shock of Robert's death after the meeting, but I must say Michael's win came just at the right time.

>> The funeral cortège of Robert Dunlop travels down the country road near Ballymoney, where he lived in Co. Antrim.

≫ Robert Dunlop's sisters, Linda, Helen, Virginia and Margaret (hidden), carry his coffin as his sons Michael and William walk alongside during his funeral at Garryduff Presbyterian Church.

Michael meantime made it clear that he was a TT enthusiast, just like his father; but there was a lot of heartache and some serious decisions to be made before he raced. "A few days after Dad's funeral everyone had left home, including William and Daniel, my other brother. I was on my own, sitting in the garage and deeply depressed, waiting for something to happen which was not happening.

"People were calling at the house to pay their respects and then naturally went home. I know that they all meant well, but it was getting me down listening to all the stories. I decided I wasn't doing the TT, as my mother was having a bad time at home then.

"I missed Dad shouting at me to get up in the morning. I would just try and lie in bed all day, then he would come and drag me out of it. I would shout back at him, which I regret now. I really do miss him. We weren't such a close family as you could find elsewhere, but deep down we all knew that we loved one another.

<< "Well done, son!" Michael Dunlop is congratulated on winning the Manx Grand Prix Newcomers' Race by his father, Robert, who also won the Newcomers' Manx twenty-three years before, in 1983.

"It's a pity we didn't have a sister for my mother, as it must have been a nightmare bringing us up. Thankfully there were neighbours and my girlfriend, Jill Attley, who came round the house and were there nearly every night. My mother is into her horses, and I know nothing about them; I normally kept out of the way.

"When the TT practice started I sat in my garage listening to it on the radio, and this got me more depressed. I sat down with Mum and chatted about me racing, and she indicated that she didn't want me to go but told me to do what I wanted. This didn't answer any questions in my mind, so I went outside and pulled everything out of the van, which was still packed up from the North West 200.

>> Robert Dunlop crosses the line and takes the win in the 125cc class, his fifteenth win at the famous circuit during the 2007 North West 200.

"As I started to put things back in the garage I thought of the tools I would need for the TT and left them to one side. As the hours passed I decided I could pack the van up just in case Mum told me to go.

"My friends and sponsors were all behind me, but there wasn't a ferry until Wednesday evening, so I was going to miss more practice. Then Paul Phillips from the TT phoned to say that Wednesday practice was cancelled, so there was no rush and to just get the normal ferry. With the van sitting in our yard all ready to go I sat in the garage waiting for a signal. I just wanted Mum to come out of the house and tell me to look after himself, or Dad to knock down one of the spanners off the wall. As time passed there was no obvious answer, and the deadline for getting the ferry was dangerously close and I still had to race to Newry in Co. Down to pick up the fuel.

> That's when I decided I was no longer a little boy and made the decision I was a man and should make my own move. I was off to the TT.

"That's when I decided I was no longer a little boy and made the decision I was a man and should make my own move. I was off to the TT."

Dunlop eventually achieved a better placing than might have been hoped for in view of the circumstances; but, knowing the family's link with the Isle of Man, there is no doubt that Michael will fill a higher placing than tenth when he goes to races next year.

In retrospect, it was a superb performance, not only to win at the North West but to compete in the TT at all. He must have been on an adrenalin rush. His performance was a gritty one, to say the least.

Robert Dunlop, the greatest North West racer of all time, warms up his bike on the grid during 2007 practice.

And what of Louise, the woman who was left to pick up the pieces? Louise had always been at Robert's side and had looked favourably on the boys racing. In many ways she was pleased—one might even say relieved—that Michael and William decided to carry on. Who can say what's ahead of her? And the fact that she is involved in show horses gives her another sideline, which she desperately needed after Robert's death, to lift her mind if nothing else.

Is she still anxious when William and Michael go racing? Of course she is, but she knows they must do what they have to do. Robert was of the same nature, for racing was in his blood, and there was no way he was going to change.

Louise, of course, misses him badly. "There's a coat over the door in the garage, which is Robert's coat. I haven't moved it. I still feel I'll see his face pop up and ask me for a cup of tea."

Robert Dunlop sits beside the stove as the kettle boils in his Ballymoney home.

> Robert Dunlop begins an unofficial test session on the road outside his home in Ballymoney.

ISLE OF MAN TT

Number of race wins:	**5**
Number of podiums:	**14**
Number of second places:	**3**
Number of third places:	**6**
Number of TT races started:	**38**
Number of TT finishes:	**28**
Number of DNFs [did not finish]:	**10**

First TT win: 1989 (debut race)

1989:	125cc TT win and new lap record (103.02mph)
1990:	125cc TT win and new lap record (104.09mph)
1991:	125cc TT win and new lap record (106.71mph)
1991:	250cc Junior win and fastest lap in race (114.27mph)
1998:	125cc TT win
1998:	Fastest recorded lap for a 125cc machine in Wednesday night practice (112.11mph)

ROLL OF HONOUR RACE WINS

North West 200 **15**

125cc:	1990, 1991, 1993, 1994, 2006
250/1:	1991, 1993
250/2:	1992, 1993
350cc:	1986
SBK/1:	1990, 1991, 1994
SBK/2:	1990, 1994

Isle of Man TT **5**

125cc:	1989, 1990, 1991, 1998
250cc:	1991

Ulster Grand Prix **9**

125cc:	1990, 1991, 1993, 1998, 2000, 2001, 2003
SBK/1:	1992
SBK/2:	1992

Dundrod 150 **8**

125cc:	1984, 1987, 1989, 1990, 1998, 2003, 2006, 2007

Irish National RR **111** (1980–2008)

Cookstown 100:	**11**
Tandragee 100:	**7**
Killinchy 150 / Dundrod 150:	**8**
Temple 100:	**6**
Mid-Antrim 150:	**14**
Monaghan:	**2**
Carrowdore 100:	**8**
Sligo 100:	**3**
Athea:	**4**
Skerries:	**13**
Race of the South:	**14**
Kells:	**4**
Faugheen 0:	**2**
Dundalk:	**4**
Killalane:	**11**

Sunflower **7**

125cc:	1986, 1989, 1991, 1993
125/2:	1993
250cc:	1985
350cc:	1985

Isle of Man National RR **13**

Manx Grand Prix Junior Newcomer:	1993
Southern 100:	**10**
Steam Packet:	**2**

Irish SC Championship **18**

125cc:	**14**
250cc:	**1**
F2:	**1**
1,000cc:	**2**

World F1	0	3rd:	1989, 3rd: 1990, 3rd: 1998
World F2	0	19th:	1986
European 125cc	0	12th:	1993, 13th: 1992
		Race win, Kirkistown: 1993	
Belgian 125cc	0	6th:	2001
British Superbike	0	2nd:	1992
MCN Superbike	0	3rd:	1992
		Race win, Cadwell Park	
British 125cc	1		1991
Irish Road Race	11	125cc:	1982, 1985, 1987, 1993, 2001, 2003, 2006, 2007
		250cc:	1985
		350cc:	1987
		1,000cc:	1987
Ulster Road Race	6	125cc:	1982, 1985, 1986, 1987
		250cc:	1985
		1,000cc:	1987
Southern Road Race	1	125cc:	2006
Irish Short Circuit	1	125cc:	2006
Ulster Short Circuit	2	125cc:	1983, 1986
John Player 125cc	1		1986
Shell 125cc	0	5th:	1993
Superkings 125cc	0	3rd:	1998
Two-Stroke Racing S-Club	2	125cc:	2006, 2007

Frohburg	1	125cc:	2004
Mettet Grand Trophy	1	125cc:	2001
Macau Grand Prix	1		1989 (2nd: 1988, 1993)
Indonesian Grand Prix	1		1993
Welsh Open	1		1991
Enkalon Trophy	1		1989
Mondello Race of the Year	1		1984

Ralph Rensen Trophy, 1985, 1987
Enkalon Irish Motorcyclist of the Year, 1987, 1991
Diploma of Outstanding Merit (Joey Dunlop Trophy), 1997
Honorary doctorate, University of Ulster, 2006
Honorary freedom of the borough of Ballymoney, 2006

Robert Dunlop receives his University of Ulster Honorary Doctorate in 2006.

Robert Dunlop receives his Honorary Freedom of the Borough of Ballymoney in 2006.

Robert Dunlop with Giacomo Agostini at the Centenary TT Champions Gala Dinner in the Isle of Man in 2007.